Unimaginatively Western World!

What Makes Immigrant Parents Struggles to Raise their Children in Western World?

Majok Wutchok

Bor Publishers

Copyright © By Majok Wutchok

All rights reserved. No part of this guide may be reproduced in any form without permission in writing from the publisher except in the case of brief quotations embodied in critical articles or reviews.

ISBN: 978-0-6482848-1-9

This edition published by Bor Publishers, 2018.

Legal & Disclaimer

The information contained in this book and its contents is not designed to replace or take the place of any form of medical or professional advice; and is not meant to replace the need for independent medical, financial, legal or other professional advice or services, as may be required. The content and information in this book has been provided for educational and empowerment purposes only.

The content and information contained in this book has been compiled from sources deemed reliable, and it is accurate to the best of the Author's knowledge, information and belief. However, the Author cannot guarantee its accuracy and validity and cannot be held liable for any errors and/or omissions. Further, changes are periodically made to this book as and when needed. Where appropriate and/or necessary, you must consult a professional (including but not limited to your doctor, attorney, financial advisor or such other professional advisor) before using any of the suggested remedies, techniques, or information in this book.

Upon using the contents and information contained in this book, you agree to hold harmless the Author from and against any damages, costs, and expenses, including any legal fees potentially resulting from the application of any of the information provided by this book. This disclaimer applies to any loss, damages or injury caused by the use and application, whether directly or indirectly, of any advice or information presented, whether for breach of contract, tort, negligence, personal injury, criminal intent, or under any other cause of actions.

DEDICATION

This short book is an inspirational dedication to my three children namely; Achol, Kur, De'Von Deng and our special person, Eunice.

Table of Contents

PROLOGUE V

INTRODUCTION VII

CHAPTER 1 1
POVERTY 1

CHAPTER 2 7
IMMIGRATION OF AFRICANS TO AUSTRALIA: SUCCESS OF AFRICANS REFUGEES VERSE BRAIN DRAINS BOOSTING AUSTRALIA ECONOMY 7

CHAPTER 3 15
STEREOTYPING OF AFRICAN MINORITIES BY THE AUSTRALIAN MEDIA 15

CHAPTER 4 21
RACISM AND JOB SEGREGATION AGAINST AFRICAN MINORITIES IN AUSTRALIA 21

CHAPTER 5 32
YOUTH CRIMES AND FAKE APEX GANGS IN MELBOURNE ... 32

CHAPTER 6 39
MULTILINGUALISM 39

CHAPTER 7 46
JOB INSECURITY AND DIFFICULTY IN SECURING SHELTER 46

CHAPTER 8 52
FEAR OF DEPORTATION 52

CHAPTER 9 58
   OVERREPRESENTATION 58

CHAPTER 10 64

   ACCESS TO BASIC AMENITIES 64

CHAPTER 11 76
   DISCRIMINATION, STIGMATISATION AND RACISM 76

CHAPTER 12 83
   CULTURAL EXPECTATIONS 83

CONCLUSION 89

Reference 91

PROLOGUE

Immigration is gradually becoming a norm in the western countries; individuals and families migrate to most western countries for greener pastures. The problem experienced by minority racial or ethnic groups with families is more complex than that of a single person. This book highlights and explicitly discusses the challenges that immigrant parents either documented or undocumented face alongside their children in a foreign land. The difference in cultural and social lifestyle is a potential factor that contributes to intra-family crisis and conflicts. Most immigrants fail to be aware of other factors that may hinder the comfort and settling in the host country. From the issues that concerns basic needs of human being, to the fear of being deported, to the issues of multilingualism and different cultural expectations is pointed out and helpful hints to help parents best understand and interact with their children. This book also address the issue of parents knowing how to dialogue and communicate with their children as well as be a positive influence to their children and ultimately change the world's perspective against racism and discrimination.

INTRODUCTION

This book titled *"Unimaginatively Western World! What Makes Immigrant Parents Struggles to Raise their Children in Western World"* explicitly discuss about the difficulties immigrants face in the western world most especially immigrants with children. Initially, most immigrants consider their new environment as a safe haven, better opportunity only for it to soon become a dreadful nightmare just upon their arrival, when it comes to raising their kids and saving their cultural heritage. The challenges encountered by immigrants are complex and immense, hence the need to break it down into chapters for better comprehension.

Challenges that are as a result of conflict between main cultural practices of immigrants which chaperons' one of the core and universal obligations i.e. parenting – raising a child. For instance, in the country the immigrant migrated from, it is a common practice to discipline children accordingly. However, from the moment of migration, the disciplinary methods adopted from the immigrant's country may be completely prohibited in the new country migrated into. This may lead to the involvement of authorities in charge of Child Protection, escalating issues that happen to be a minor issue to the immigrant i.e. immigrants is not familiar with the kind of protocol that exists in the country to settle the supposed family dispute.

Oblivious of the laws guiding the country as regards Child Protection, this may pose a great danger of temporary or permanent separation of immigrant parent and a child, homelessness arose, crimes became imminent, imprisonment arose, Child Protection failing their roles, police brutality arose, media houses segregation becomes norms, vilification as a reality in immigrants communities, immigration detentions kicked-in and deportation occurs illegally. Panic, anxiety and mistrust for parents is expected when an immigrant parent is faced with a case considered as minute disciplinary issue warrants a case file opened with a Child Protection Service agent. Consequently, this book's twelve short chapters explicitly focuses on some major challenges and drawbacks faced by immigrant parents and their children from economic stability, access to service utilisation, shelter, a better paying job, and generally a better opportunity hoped for when leaving their homeland.

Psychological and emotional related issues are also being faced by parents and children of immigrants, take for instance the child bullying and stigmatisation encountered by children in schools is reported to the immigrant parent, there is little to nothing to be done in this case than to report to the school authority. Most African immigrants especially are faced with stigmatisation, in cases where an immigrated Nigerian or Somali child is stigmatised for terrorism or cyber-crime, a South Sudanese child is stigmatised for Australian media's fabricated word "African Gang" asides being considered inferior due to his or her skin colour. In addition to facing a more than likely chance of bullying or external hostility, it is expected of most immigrant children to deal oftentimes with mini aggressions due to their choice of clothing, social life, food, manners, religion and etc. The term 'different' and 'fit in' are frequently used by these kids to explain their emotional traumas encountered at school to their parent.

Unfortunately, most immigrant parents neglects this complaints and warnings from their children and tend to focus more on academic triumphs and wants their kids to make a better opportunity of their new country and also focus on other issues that concerns their survival. Few chapters of this book will further go into details of how it came about and how immigrant parents can identify and swiftly attend and act on the social needs of their offspring. The most encountered challenge occurs during the adolescent stage of the immigrant children. Parents will want their ward to maintain their cultural values; on the other hand, the child seeking for ways to fit in and be accepted amongst their peers tends to be vulnerable to severe depression, rebellion and isolation at this stage. Particularly when issues like whom to date, clothing, and adapted lifestyle the immigrant parents are questioning; this may result into a distraught and disturbing reaction from the child.

The price of posterity i.e. the maintenance of cultural values and custom is a difficult one for most immigrant parents as more compromise is being made than expected. It is therefore imperative for immigrant parent to learn to be flexible and compassionate in order not to jeopardise the future of their lifestyle and cherished culture. Acceptance, validation and encouragement are required in order to excel and live a fulfilled, happy and organised life. The provision of this kind of support at home provides the children as well as the parents the confidence and assurance needed to battle the prejudice and learn to accept and love their cultural background, as that is who they really are. One chapter discusses explicitly and extensively the cultural expectations as well as tips to on how to help immigrant parents to swiftly attend to cultural misconceptions and derailment, most especially when the child feels the need to be accepted.

Economic woes oftentimes referred to as poverty, is a major factor that contributes majorly to the struggles immigrant parents face to nurture their child in a new country. Immigrant children who are faced with money problems are more likely to suffer acute depressive symptoms in schools most especially children in their adolescent stage. In addition, the issue of poverty may not make a difference even when a paying job is secured, as language barrier may be an issue. Multilingualism may pose as a hindrance to making more, as the lack of fluency in the native language of the country migrated into may result into more effort less payment. In the first instance, before immigrant parent(s) can attain financial stability it will take a while except if not faced with money problems, several menial jobs will be taken, for instance a former small company manager becomes a factory worker. In the United States, several menial jobs are taken mostly by migrated foreigners includes, janitors, gardeners, factory works, truck drivers etc. Chapter 7 discusses into details securing shelter and job security for immigrant parents to best support their family.

Although the cause of these struggles may be emotionally and psychologically related, it is expedient to learn the cause as well as the tips to help identify and curb the situation. Charities, foundations, care groups and wits of a parent can help nurture a child but knowledge of these prior to immigration may save a willing immigrant from stress as an immigrant parent.

CHAPTER 1

POVERTY

The major contributing factor for migrating to other country is poverty, war, and lack of access to basic amenities, lack of better opportunity in general. Poverty as defined by the federal government of American authorities in 1964, is when a person is said to be in poverty if the pre-tax cash income of the family in which the person resides falls below the officially determined threshold, this definition is based on family size. However, each year the threshold of poverty is adjusted annually based on the current rate of inflation. (Poverty and Income Centre for Immigration Studies). The rates of poverty have vast implications on the society in general and not only on the immigrant. The impact poverty has on immigrant parents result into emotional, physical and mental distress. Unfortunately, most immigrant parents particularly the illegal immigrants, are at a disadvantage following the fear of deportation making them acclaim the principle of more effort less payment.

Most times, the wages earned are minimal as compared to the work done; this has a negative impact on the child of the immigrant in the sense that little time will be dedicated to the child. This case may be worse if the immigrant happens to be a single parent, this is because of the profound impact it has on the parent-child relationship, most especially when it comes to spending quality time. As compared to traditional parenting, an immigrant single parent is less likely to be associated with better life outcome simply because the sole responsibility of welfare is on one person. Better life outcome such as emotional wellbeing, financial success, career development and better accomplishment educationally for child and adult is easier in traditional families i.e. both parent. Although there is a potential of having high employment rates as an immigrant, however, the wages earned are not substantial as compared to an indigene of the country, worse is the immigrant has a lesser chance of benefitting from the work supports of government. In addition to this, the child of an immigrant is also less likely to gain access to programs scheduled for the prekindergarten like the indigene.

According to the data gathered by the United States Census Bureau, the main reason immigrant parents are constantly associated with financial woes is because of their lack of education. About 29 per cent of immigrant parent is yet to complete high school, and a larger proportion has less than high school education. Therefore, poorly educated immigrants are more likely to start procreating earlier than a semi or well-educated immigrant. In spite of the high poverty level, immigrant parents with children have a minimal chance of receiving welfare benefits from government such as food stamps or cash welfare payments.

Unfortunately, the case of child poverty that poses an important social problem is linked to underprivileged socioeconomic outcomes in adulthood, which causes schooling problems and prolonged developmental complications on the child. The marital status as well as the pattern of employment of the immigrant parent's links strongly to child poverty. Evidently, the neighbourhood of the immigrant tends to have few obvious distinctive features that differentiate it from the rest of the neighbouring communities, which acts as a contributing factor to the struggles encountered by an immigrant parent, most especially a single parent. Mental health cases are reported less frequently in the children of immigrants from poor families, this may be due to parental depression, ineffective parenting and family dysfunction in rare cases.

Even though, it is expected for immigrants to experience poverty, unemployment and underemployment in the first few years of resettlement, however the expectations that the phase is only temporary will help the immigrant family stay together. Even if the immigrant parents successfully adapts into the new environment, the impact of staying poor is the negative effect that reflects on the child which may include negative impact on child's IQ, internalised problems, school achievement as well as outward behaviours. Compared with impoverished families, transiently poor families are less likely to experience greater financial stress, parental depression as well as familial discord. The impoverished poor families are more open to harsh disciplinary methods on their kids.

In 2009, the immigrants in the American suburbs experienced a notable higher poverty rates than native-born. Then, living in the suburbs was concomitant with greater economic and financial well being than residing in the cities of USA regardless of origin. The poverty rate among the natives of America living in the suburbs was lesser than those residing in the cities to which this significant gap was obvious amongst immigrants as well. (Roberto, *et al.* 2011). Just as the cause of poverty, the welfare and comfort in the suburbs of America was as a result of the combination social, demographic and economic factors. Immigrants with better skill set and education functions and thrive better in the suburbs, in return they and their children benefits from available healthcare, public safety, and utilisation of better services, transportation, and educational services in the suburb. In addition, the immigrants create and utilise economic opportunities away from the urban cities.

In the bid to settle in quickly and comfortably in the early years of migration, most immigrants are plagued with loneliness and depression especially where there are few people with the same socio-cultural heritage to relate with

(Ponizovsky and Ritsner, 2004). It is expedient for service providers to take this as a condition in itself most particularly for child welfare so as not to result into parental isolation, which is mostly as a result of maltreatment of the child. This is imperative and essential because the attention of service providers such as child protection or child support until the attention of a third party is drawn and calls the notice of the service providers.

Therefore, in order to curb future menace to the society by raising children by struggling due to poverty, adequate knowledge of the rules of the country should be understood. Workable skills set should be acquired and perfected as it is established that in the suburbs, immigrant families tend to survive based on level of education as well as skill set to be able to gain their fit and blend in quickly. Raising a child in poverty as an immigrant parent is far less stressful than that of a single parent.

CHAPTER 2

IMMIGRATION OF AFRICANS TO AUSTRALIA: SUCCESS OF AFRICANS REFUGEES VERSE BRAIN DRAINS BOOSTING AUSTRALIA ECONOMY.

The population of African community in Australia is ever growing. The immigration of Africans into Australia has been both as a refugee via the humanity program of Australia and larger immigrants migrated via the skilled or economic immigrants and family reunion system of Australia. Africa as a continent is not particularly strange to many contradictions; the presence of several inhumane inconvenience and bad government decisions has resulted into many immigrating into another country. The cause of political instability and conflict maybe the combination of natural disaster as well as manmade issues.

The coping mechanism and survival strategy many indigenous Africans have seemed to adopt due to unstable climatic, political, social, religious, environmental and economic conditions is moving from their nation to another with more stable political systems. The issue of immigration has resulted into many Africans contribute to the high increase in population mobility and the most mobile community in the world (Findley, 1997; Adepoju, 1997). All African countries are different in respect to their language, lifestyle, culture, socioeconomic, history and political background. These diversities are the same way the Australian relationship with each Africans follow the dynamic.

The relationship between Africans and Australians dated as far back as 1861, during the era of slave trade, colonialism, some African citizen were moved involuntarily to Australia while some others were natively born in Europe and into Australia as a native (Jakubowicz, 2010). Following the achievement of independence, each country the affiliation of the African country and that of the Australian government continued at the government level, to which the African students were permitted to study in any authorised university in Australia. As part of improvement assistance program, the Australian government granted scholarships to nations such as Sudan and Eritrea, in order to increase skilled manpower. However, during this time the political instability of these countries heightened thereby resulting into students staying back to establish themselves in Australia.

This chapter discusses and argues about the positive impact successful refugees and brain drained Africans contribute to the economic situation of Australia. Many of these migrants, when equipped with skills ensures that they utilise it to the very best as most times, it is difficult to secure a better opportunity in terms of job security except in some rare cases where the qualification and experience of the migrant speaks for itself and place the migrant in a better position. A lot of Australians are still sluggishly behind not accepting the fact that Australia has benefited handsomely from Africa. The humanitarian and skilled migrations have contributed to Australian wider economy successful in most sectors of the economic. Most Sudan/South Sudanese born populations have acquired higher education and gained entry into the job market competitively in mostly resources sector, healthcare sector, community services and manufacturing industry. Those in labour workforce have majority of them holding degrees but had been forced by circumstances like systemic segregation that doesn't recognise them they're professionals of Australia, so they take ups what comes their way to support their families. South Sudanese Community has produced highly competitive lawyers, medical doctors, public health professionals, medical scientists, psychologists, social workers, nurses, many accountants, economists, major banks consultants, huge mine engineers and many more. They in other hands invested heavily in children education mostly in private educational sector and property markets. Mainstream is not accepting Africans, but Aussies with media brainwashed are getting caught by surprises that, African Australians are moving forwards despite racial profiling and barbaric calling of African names by politicians in Canberra, the resilience some Africans had either collapse of economic in their own country of origin or during wars time and living refugee lifestyles for instance, South Sudanese war have made everyone in their community very strong to deal with any life situations. African Australians have been called anything, thrown raw eggs, verbally abused on the streets of Australia but they are unshakeable and unbeatable by those misinformed Australians. The largest component of Australia's migration system is its Skills Stream, to which there are different groups within the Skill Stream, they include;

- Employer Supported immigrant: in which immigrants are employed and supported by employers.
- Business Skilled Entry: in which successful business moguls or tycoons migrate to Australia.
- State Supported immigrant: in which territory and state government acknowledge and recognize shortages of skills.
- Famous Talent Visas: these are issued to individuals with unique or special talents of significant benefit to Australia.

With these Skill Stream program several Africans migrated from their homeland to Australia especially Africans from Eastern and Southern Africa. All regions of Africa is accounted for the Skills Stream to which the largest groups of immigrants were professionals i.e. successful and qualified experts who see it profitable for them and their children to migrate into Australia. Medical practitioners, Nurses, Mining engineers and Accountants accounts for most professionals who migrate into Australia. Australia has expressively gained from the ever-growing African-born society. On the other hand, while the outcome of skilled migration is a net advantage to Australia, this is not mostly achieved in the country of origin.

A fraction of the brain drain Australia benefits from is the human resources tutoring and development paid for by ill-resourced African countries but the benefit of the work is enjoyed by Australia. For instance, according to research and statistics put together by DEEWR circa 2008, Africa forfeited 577 nurses and 359 qualified doctors to Australia. Another debate could possible emerge stating ill-resourced African countries train more than needed nurses and in exchange of foreign exchange the surplus nurses are being moved to Australia. However, it is almost impossible for Africa as a continent to have a tendency of having surplus medical practitioners.

So, if Australia is to receive medical physicians emigrating from any African country, serious consideration is to be put on responsibility for influencing the training of the replacement of the received physicians. In addition, African countries can as well benefit from skilled migration, which is the remittance being sent home by professionals working in Australia to their relations back in their homeland. The remittance plays a major role in economic development by improving the condition of living and establishment of small business in rural areas for sustenance. Although difficult to accurately quantify, these remittances are a huge foundation of foreign exchange for African countries.

Also, in some cases, remittances are estimated to signify as much as five per cent of the GDP of countries in Arica with the overall transfers estimated to reach as much as $40 billion per annum. Australian Refugee council noted that this both surpasses official development aid to the region, and in many countries surpasses foreign direct investment too. Remittance and the activities related to it go beyond simply sending funds to relatives in their homeland. Africans in Australia also have contributed and donated huge funds to their respective homeland through several government aids and international welfare. For instance, the community of Ethiopians in Australia contributed to the Fistula Foundation of Australia of about thousands of dollars. Likewise, the communities of Africans in Australia donated reliefs and funds through programs such as Care Australia to tackle health related issues in rural areas of African countries.

Consequently, many migrants considered Australia as an insurance strategy conducted unconventionally of kinship networks. The policy of Australian immigration has progressively designed to maximise economic and human capital as well as implement the brain drain most Africans were bothered about. Australia has been progressively successful in bagging high percentage of successful experts and brain drains in managerial and professional positions from most African countries.

CHAPTER 3
STEREOTYPING OF AFRICAN MINORITIES BY THE AUSTRALIAN MEDIA

Asides the cluelessness of natives of Australia about Africa as a continent, most natives mistakes Africa as a country and all Africans to be from the same homeland. Several Africans from different country has encountered stereotyping one way or the other either at school, parks, workplace or any social gathering. The dehumanising manner in which the European and American colonialism brought towards the exposure of Africa and its culture contributes to the stereotyping as well as racist interaction that most western world including Australia projects the image of Africa. In addition, the indolent depiction of Africa by the media alongside lack of exposure contributes greatly to the ignorance of Australia towards Africa. However, with the level of exposure and information the Internet seems to possess, it shows evidently through social inclusions that stereotyping is due to the decision not to care.

The result of media stereotyping has led to several issues of inferiority complex amongst children of immigrant in their respective institution of learning as well as migrant parent at their respective workplace or social gathering. For instance, An Australian native expects a South Sudanese to expressively claim being African than causing a huge hassle being specific by claiming his or her generic background. Therefore, causing complex confusions by calling a South Sudanese native and a Kenyan native to be from the same environs. The culture of African American is well recognised in the contemporary society and has a major influence in social media, movies and music. This has affected several Africans in Australia due to the stereotypic mentality that accompanies it. Several Australian seems to think they have all black skinned Africans figured out due to what the American media i.e. Talk shows, reality TV series, movies, music concerts of black Americans etc. portrays.

Similarly, the stereotypes of most African American as affected directly or indirectly the behaviour of black Africans in Australia. The culture of the African American is what is most recognised and accepted, hence, resulting into the mimic of the stereotypical behaviour and mannerisms of African Australians. This is most evident in the lifestyles of African teenagers in Australia, in order to fit in; this behaviour is adopted for social approval. The pressure being faced by teenagers to belong often result into the confusion of identity and pretence to be who they are not. Australia as a nation prides itself on being down to earth and original. Every native Australian claims to value fairness, fair go, therefore when African minorities in Australia are being marginalised and speaks out against forces of tyranny and when the idea of fairness is being questioned, Australian natives shy away from it.

Several misconceptions created by the stereotypical views of Australian media against African minorities have led to different kinds of insecurities in social inclusion, peer-to-peer relationship as well as within educational institutions. The need to feel safe imperatively arises in the hearts of younger migrants of the African minority in Australia. Just as some African countries are stereotypically known for bombing, terrorism, malnutrition, deadly diseases and etc., this poses a great danger to social acceptance and interaction. The violent images put forward by the media shapes the mindset of Aussies as regards social inclusion of African minorities. These stereotypes from the media are often exaggerated and remain oblivious of the fear and anxiety faced by majority of African minorities, as they are mostly victims of terror and racism. Australian media has the tendency to exclude the cultural, political as well as social forums of African Australians especially, what places emphasis on the importance of comprehending due to the negative nature of the treatment of the Australian media indigenous minority media. According to Cover, 2012, which states the imperative need to promote the analysis of ways to which immigrant groups utilise media to deliver spaces for the articulation and construction of their concepts and opinions of politics, identity and community and also the comprehension of larger society and their position in it.

Identifying and comprehending African minority media can help realise to what degree minority concerns are able to locate and discover platforms to which majority public sphere and range to which marginalised members of society are able to be heard, seen and well understood. According to the report that followed a festival held in Melbourne circa 2017, the media published images that alleged African Australian youths as perpetrators of the incident. However, according to reports from the Police which states the incidents erupted from youth of several backgrounds not particularly the African Australians. Either by commission or by omission, the coverage of the known Apex gang by the media intensifies the racial stereotypes about African Australians with black skins. In cases whereby an African American is apprehended for a crime, rather than the term 'accused or alleged offender', the word 'thug' is used in place of it.

The perceptions and use of racial descriptors is nerve-wracking, headlines given to related crimes for African minorities are quite different from Caucasians from other continent. This is quite difficult for immigrant parents and children of African heritage to live an enjoyable life that was foreseen in their homeland. Immigrants from Sudan and South Sudan living in Australia are the ones feeling the heat of stereotypes the most as they are portrayed 'problematic and quite hard to fit in' by the media.

CHAPTER 4

RACISM AND JOB SEGREGATION AGAINST AFRICAN MINORITIES IN AUSTRALIA

The issue with racism and job segregation challenges faced by African minorities in Australia is fast becoming a major concern to the country. Rather than castigating and segregating native Australians from African Australian during a job interview, it is more advantageous to support the social inclusion most African minorities strive for.

Australia as a land of enormous opportunities had given most immigrants so many privileges to establish their lives but in the other hand, the Australian society is full of bigotry people, races people who are unbelievably uncomfortable with the immigration policies that had allowed people like myself who are Africans and are South Sudanese in particular to prosper in their land. Being an African in Australia, you are judged by what you didn't do. South Sudanese youth are among the top immigrants who have earned higher education degrees in Australia but still they are denied jobs based on their professions due to being labeled as lacking experience to the professional industry. Where will they get experience if they're not given opportunities to show their practicalities on University knowledge gained? They got educated in Australia and they are Australians, where do they go to get experience from? Australia is the country where immigrants worked in the factories with higher university qualifications but in mainstream society, you find executives with certificates and diplomas taking over top jobs, something that tells you that you are unwanted and unworthy in Australia. When I first came to Australia as a refugee, I knew Australia would be a land of opportunities and a land full of so many struggles. The first event I had encountered was, when we catch a bus going to Adelaide city centre on Sunday morning of November 2003 to attend Dinka congregation church service, we entered in the bus and we inserted our bus cards in bus card scan machine, inside the bus there were few seats available. We sat on one seat opposite the other facing us, two couples at their 40s were sitting opposite to us too. The bus keeps on going whilst frequently stopping to pick up more passengers, on one next stop, the bus was full to the brim and a lot of people were standing and the funny thing was that, on our seat we had one more space and no one seem to come and sit next to the black men. The couples opposite our seat didn't want to make an eyes contact due to their own paranoid attitudes and their mindsets. One guy started conversing with his partner that, where are these stupid baboons coming from? He asked his partner? The partner responded mysteriously, what the fuck are we doing next to them? She questioned her partner back? Let's the fuck leaved them alone since everyone is ignoring their empty seat! the partner replied. We were shouting our mouths without responding to such aggressive situation, ignorance was the best solution to what we were facing. The couples saw us not responding them anything, the male partner stood up and yielded, let stand and leave the baboons in their area. He aggressively asserted! They left their seat and stood in the bus like other white fellows who didn't want to share with black men. Jok and I were only a week old in Adelaide, South Australia. After we arrived at our destination, I asked Jok, is this country we are going to live, study and work in? Jok said, yeah brother, we can resist anything until the Australians themselves give up with their attitudes towards black people. He replied and I noted it with confidence and affirmative that we must be resilience to any unforeseeable future situations as we continue to lived here. How many times I have been cruelly yielded at on streets going about my business? Called with all cruelty names and horrific racial shout-out.

How many times had my car been thrown with raw eggs? It tells you that something is amiss in Australia. Australians themselves are very races people in nature and disgrace in the way they treated immigrants especially Africans. The only imperative thing that keeps us in little respect here is the rule of law, otherwise most Australian are not great people you would prefer living with. South Sudanese families came to Australia with their way of disciplining their children, an African way where the responsibility of raising a child is based on a village raising a child. A child is disciplined when they are wrong but in Australia, children are not smack or either caned, something that had found majority of children in my community being snatched away by

Department of Child Protection agency (DCP). The children are fostered to the mainstream families with different cultures. The children are not given any priority to either go back to their parents or either to go and live with relatives. It's something that they are denied to doing, they lived in alcoholics and drugs inhibited families. Mainstream families that are unable to raise well-mannered children, they children learned those horrible habits and they act like those drugs heads families. Their biological parents and relatives are kept in dark corners to the extend where they cannot trace their children's whereabouts. The children will be mistreated, misled, mislabeled and until they becomes misfortunate and dysfunctional to their community than they are released from prisons. The DCP and the police release them when they have realise that, these young people will occasionally visited prisons, are no longer useful to their families, are mentally torturous, their well beings are abnormal and are lowest useful people, then they are released back to their respective communities. They wanted to destroy the younger generation who are growing up here within South Sudanese community in

Australia. The Australian media houses reported anything that betrays and tarnish Africans or South Sudanese community even if it's only one person's problem. The whole community is seen as evil, uncultivated, criminals, unproductive and not integrating to mainstream society. Can we really integrate into this society full of bigotry, hatred, full of racially motivated individuals, a society where people gives you fake smiles, a society where racial profiling is growing and minorities from immigrants communities are singled out by government officials? I came from a community where education is taken seriously, a community where people lived communally and help those in needs, a community where people of my age are highly well educated, thanks Australian government for that. A community, where majority of my age are very competitive in establishing their families, buying properties and investing in their children educations. Is this the community that most people in Australia targeted and tarnished by the wrong deeds of some bad apples that were born here, grew up here and adapt those Australian strange behaviours, which are unAfrican? We are not who most Australians think we're. South Sudanese are great people, people who are very intelligently driven by opportunities.

Acknowledgement of qualification, success and experience as well as celebrating success by creating avenues to help boost Australian economy is more of a priority than segregating and pulling out the racist card when considering the ethnic minority for a job position. Also, huge efforts are required to make sure that institutions especially the police imitate the multicultural composition of Australia. The economy of Australia is expected to be unstable if employers reduce the ethnic minority of African Australians to major stereotypes based mainly on appearance. Rather, potential employers should connect the massive social, cultural and economic potential of the Australians of Africa background to the fullest. This takes effect when one begins to stimulate the response and perception of newly arrived migrants with comprehension rather than with a clutched fist.

As discovered by the Human Rights Commission of Australia, that Australians of Africa background faces major discrimination when seeking employment and shelter, which has resulted into social exclusion.

However, the attitude of racism in Australia is persistent. For instance, there is a high rate of discrimination or segregation on most consumer-focused job (e.g. waiters), which I more consistent to an extent of consumer-based discrimination. Nonetheless, consumer discrimination is not the sole reason for racism, discrimination and job segregation. Other factors that contribute to racism and job segregation may include the taste-based discrimination by employers or colleagues at work or simply statistical discrimination. Individuals from refugee or migrant background in Australia are discovered to be the ones given the lowest level of jobs regardless of skill, experience and qualification (Colic-Peisker & Tilbury 2005).

Individuals from refugee and developing communities have been discovered to be susceptible to discrimination, which is often the case with individuals whom are considered to be physically different in appearance (Colic-Peisker & Tilbury 2006; HREOC 1991; 1999). The effects of race and ethnic-based discrimination are not limited to those openly subjected to it. The result of this racism can bring about climate of anxiety and fear that may restrain the activities as well as aspirations, and have emotional impact on the mental health and wellbeing of other ethnic minorities of different African countries in Australia (Szalacha et al 2003).

Several studies have found that children of African migrants are affected by race-based or ethnic discrimination, which result into higher risk of emotional and behavioural issues (Caughy, O'Campo & Muntaner 2004; Mays, Cochran & Barnes 2007). Race-based and ethnic discrimination disturbing one generation can also compromise the economic and social prospects of imminent generation, which influences intergenerational cycles of disadvantage and poverty. In addition, racism and ethnic based discrimination can destabilise positive intercultural relationships and community cohesion. In the midst of young people, it has been discovered to be known with peer violence, which at worst may result into large-scale community violence and conflicts (Forrest & Dunn 2007).

Furthermore, the rates of call back after interview is said to be discriminatory towards Australians with African background. In as much as there is evidential discrimination in the choice of interviews for entry-level jobs in Australia, the discriminatory method observes the starting point of the process of employment as choice of interview, hence, it is quite not certain to give a say in the second phase of receiving job offers. Supposing an individual's background is linked with some unidentified creative trait, there is likelihood to observe difference in outcome of the economy is sure to reflect rather than segregation and discrimination. It's unimaginatively argued that, young intellectuals of African background are intensifying changing their traditional African names to that of "Peter Dutton" in order to secure an opportunity for interview when they are applying for career jobs in Australia.

The process of job searching plays a major role in reinforcing, shaping and often time counteract inequality in Australia labour market. In the same vein, racism, segregation and other barriers to employment should be reflected to comprehend fully the generation of labour market inequality. Also, as the comparison of race suggests the way individuals adapt to obstacles of workplace can take diverse turn and have clear consequences. Therefore, it is imperative to systematically examine and scrutinise job search and also behaviours of segregation as well as other limitations in the workplace in order to fully comprehend and correct pervasive racial inequalities in the Australian labour market.

CHAPTER 5
YOUTH CRIMES AND FAKE APEX GANGS IN MELBOURNE

Youth crime in Australia is fast becoming a thing of concern as the security of life and belongings is subjected to potential threat. However, according to the Australian security forces especially the Victoria police in Melbourne reported that youth crimes are mostly perpetuated by the Caucasian youth at a higher percentage than the African Australian youth in Melbourne. Following a recent iteration that erupted during the Moomba festival circa 2016, several youth of African background specifically Sudanese natives were allegedly accused and apprehended for being the perpetrators of the violent attack. They are referred to as the APEX gang in Melbourne, the APEX gang is just a symbol intimidation word, fabricated for commercial gains by media and it does not exist. It is more or less a call sign, anti-social brand, graffiti tag and a unifying symbol. On the other hand, the police reportedly stressed the issue of using the term 'gang' which overstates the issue, also that the problem is just an on-going problem and not an ever growing issue. Also, the police state the supposed gang is not predominantly Africans. This does not rule out the existence of crime committed by African Australian youth in Melbourne and also does not discount the seriousness of the crime committed by the fake Apex gang.

Evidenced by the confession of an alleged member of the APEX gang, the issue of the riot hat escalated during the Moomba festival was blown out of proportion by the Australian media. Lack of school supports, Child Protection snatching strategy, weak parenting weaken by systemic police and Child Protection agency and unemployment led to youths and teenagers forming groups like that of Fake Apex. It is expected that as teenagers, there should be few display of youthful exuberance, but if given corrective measures as well as positive programs to keep them busy, there is still more than enough opening for a second chance. The issue of overrepresentation of the Sudanese and South Sudanese in Melbourne is a misconstruction and misconception. According to several reports, the Moomba festival fiasco was between two rival groups in Melbourne and without in depth research, it was blamed on Apex. The police delineated that the groups that partook in the riot were made up of predominantly Caucasians, Indians and Pacific Islanders.

Also, there were speculations at the time that a publication groups and news networks known as the Herald Sun, 7 News Australia, Nine News and Ten News made up the false gang known as Apex, in the same year, the Herald Sun also reported that another African Australian gang is being formed. The new gang is named 'Menace to Society' this is drawn according to the evidential graffiti found at a burgled Airbnb residence as well as a few other sites. Majority of the youth crime in Australia also include alleged offenders from different country that are natives of Australia or they are Australian–born. According to crime statistics, the list of offenders recorded by the police is from Australia, New Zealand, Vietnam, India and then Sudan. With Sudan taking the least position on the least points out the overrepresentation of the African minority group. The assumption that African Australian teenagers or youth who walks together or are seated together in a park doing nothing are considered to be gangs while other racial or individuals from different countries are seen as teenagers or youth relaxing. This discriminatory act is unfair to African ethnic minority especially to the younger community who are between the ages of 10 to 24 years of age.

Therefore, the need to engage teenagers and youth in activities that helps improve their skills physically and mentally is prescribed as one of the best panacea to the issue of youth crime. The interaction with new persons helps them learn discipline and respect to others. Melbourne should take the steps Sydney took concerning declining the rate of crime, violence attacks, and gang related offences I.e. engaging the teenagers and youth in programs that keeps them off the streets and help contribute to the positive impact of the society. The Australian media coverage of crime in Melbourne increased over three high profile occurrences, which generated the awareness that gang violence is ever growing and rampant. The Victorian police informed that the assertions of gang violence are rampant are false. Although, there is a real problem with youth and teenagers of African background committing major and minor crimes in the city to which there has been no apparent increase in the level of criminal acts and persons of the African diaspora are responsible only for a segment of the crime in Melbourne.

Figure 1 below showed protest infographic made by *Majok Wutchok* to Australian media's news fabrication.

I AM NOT AN APEX GANG
MY FAMILY IS NOT APEX GANG
MY COMMUNITY HAS NO APEX GANG
APEX GANG IS A COINED UP MONEY MAKING BUSINESS STRATEGY BY 7 NEWS AND 9 NEWS NETWORKS.
WE ARE PRODUCTIVE COMMUNITY LIKE ANY OTHER COMMUNITY IN AUSTRALIA. STOP GENERALISATION, STOP VICTIMISATION
OF MY COMMUNITY.

Conclusively, it is imperative to create correctional programs and reduce the stereotypical activities peculiar to certain groups of Australian-born of different background especially the Africans. There have been several debates as regards the existence of young thugs and gangs in Melbourne by Australians, however, the police and politicians are fully convinced of the nonexistence of the group called APEX gang in Melbourne. In addition, there is a strong factor that needs to be considered, a large percentage of these supposed gangs are teenagers, who are very much likely to exude youthful exuberance. Over the years, the Australian government has continuously blamed the African minority youth living in Australia has resulting into criminal activities as their inability to integrate into the Australian society. The government has linked the problems to poverty and social issues faced by immigrants in Melbourne poor suburbs.

According to the 2016 census carried out in Australia, it is discovered that between 25 to 30 per cent of South Sudanese, Somali and Sudanese immigrants are unemployed amongst the Melbourne residents. This further contributes to the idleness of African youths living in Australia; this has laid a difference on how the government should take action to the economic challenges experienced by African migrants. The issue of blaming minorities for several societal problems will result into the perpetuation of discrimination, disempowerment and further divides members of the minority community. It is not rocket science that crime is as a result of poverty, which cannot be solved by bringing down young people's morale and locking young teenagers in cells.

CHAPTER 6
MULTILINGUALISM

Language is a competence major tool for communication and social relation, in an interpersonal sphere; it is imperative for navigating socially to family, friendship, school life and the world generally (Gleason, 1997). Immigrants as earlier portrayed are not necessarily people with minimal education or people faced with abject financial woes. There are immigrants who happens to be in a country far from their core culture and family due to work related mandate examples are organisational workers, diplomats, ambassadors, foreign officials working for multinational corporations, international organisations, corporate body such as international banks, aid workers, students etc. These set of people are also considered immigrants but mostly not used in the context of or the same way immigrants who are in search of a better opportunity who are out to secure safety in another country due to civil strife. Nonetheless, every foreign-born are considered immigrants due to difference in culture, local traditions, social class, discourse strategies and most importantly language. Certainly there are interpretation and translation agencies that offer their services to the minority of country hosting the immigrant. Conversely, the provision of incentives for the learning of the host country's language is imperative so as to pick up the pace of integration thereby lowering or eliminating the sense of segregation, alienation and insecurity felt in the beginning by immigrants. Also, there is a better advantage of bi-multilingualism. Multilingualism aggravates intercultural misunderstanding as the language barrier may pose difficulty to immigrant parents who are in search of a job. This language deficiency may cost the poor immigrant a better paying job as the potential employer may have doubt as regards the immigrant being able to comprehend and communicate to learn a trade. The inability to secure a job so as to settle in due to language barrier will result into confusion and depression and may result into a negative impact on the child. The knowledge of linguistic is paramount so as to promote mutual understanding between the native-born and the foreign born. In addition, most immigrant parents that do not possess fluency in the host country's language will have issues helping out their kids with homework and project from school most especially if the parent is a single parent with low level of education. This in turn results to the negative impact on the child's education, therefore the comprehension and fluency of the language is imperative for communication, social interaction and positive influence on the child. Academic excellence and progress of the child of the immigrant is dependent on the choice of language predominantly spoken in the home of the child

Then again, as immigrant parent multilingualism has its own bag of worries when it comes to raising your children in the host country. Reason is, the ability to be consistent on one language may prove to be quite tricky in the sense that you as a parent who wants to teach his or her child the new language; you are also particular about not losing out your mother tongue in the process. This will require such parent to think, speak and act carefully and consistently when communicating with the child.

According to traditional methods and quite a number of researches done, it is established that consistency is important. As a parent having to insist on speaking and answered back in your language is expedient as a confident level of exposure is maintained for your ward to be fluent in both your mother tongue and the host country's language. As a parent from a strict socio-cultural setting, it is vital to be quick to adapt into the new environment you find yourself in. The child of an immigrant is said to learn the language of the host country faster due to how the education system of the country is programed which makes it easier for the child to settle in better. Nevertheless, the lack of support from parent may result into isolating the child from the family, which may make the child vulnerable to the radical influences deleterious to the host country.

Sustaining the first language of the immigrant is essential for assuring access to family and public backing. Below are helpful ways a multilingual immigrant parents can help their children settle comfortably into the host country. They include:

- **Relate well with your kids**: Firsthand, you need to be able to understand relate with them as juggling between two languages may not come as easy to them as it would to you as a parent. Multilingualism in children has its advantage in life as well, you may seek out advice from others who have gone through the phase before and excelled.

- **Assist your kids with practical or reality**: converse with them and assist them with grammar rules and explain with different examples and purchase publications or literatures to best help them improve. However, for immigrants with less education, the interaction with other native-born will help in the journey of being fluent in the language of the adopted country and materials to help improve the written and spoken vocabulary of the host country should be encouraged.

- **Be flexible and Pragmatic simultaneously**: speaking a different language helps you as a parent appreciates the value of the language in itself and how it helps you survive in the host country. As you are aware, language is a primary tool of communication it warrants a parent learn how to be flexible and pragmatic to help raise multilingual parent.

The competence of the development of dual language is reliant on other factors such as the type and level of exposure as well as the age in which the child learns the second language. As a result of the assimilative forces that impels immigrant children to learn the language of the host country quickly which may pose a shift or extinction of cultural language as they begin schooling? Family, educational and clinical efforts to maintain and support the development of competence in both languages of the immigrant's child may appear to be rewarding on the long run in terms of mental wellbeing and health, cognitive advantage and educational benefits. (Toppelberg and Collins, 2010).

Oftentimes some particular working environments can impede with the cross-cultural adjustment of the immigrant parent. In a situation, where in a certain workplace where majority of the workers are of the same background linguistically which is different from the country's language, there is a tendency of apathy setting in which may pose danger making it important for immigrants to be encouraged to take better advantage of language tuition for self-improvement. As an immigrant parent to be a positive influence to your child, self-improvement in the language of the host country is crucial for social interaction and securing better opportunity.

CHAPTER 7
JOB INSECURITY AND DIFFICULTY IN SECURING SHELTER

One of the major necessities of any living thing is shelter, the same goes for human beings, while shelter shields one from harsh weather conditions, securing a comfortable job to maintain such luxury, as comfort is necessary. In Australia and Canada for instance, the immigrants face a major concerns as concerning employment, the Australian and Canadian employer refers to their credentials and experience as lacking the Australian and Canadian experience. As reported by CBC News, the Canadian government are preparing to open doors for new immigrants to whom more than half will be from the middle or economic class, while the old immigrants are still finding it a bit of a struggle to secure a job despite their highly qualified foreign credentials, domestic credentials and experience.

Unknown to many immigrants who are in the *frenzy* of new country better opportunity, there are bottle-neck opportunities that may even not fit into the job you qualify for. For instance, a certified teacher with about 15 years of teaching experience fails to secure a job that best fits into his qualification and experience and then ends up settling for what is available. However, for low-income class immigrants, the struggle for struggle for survival is not only dependent on skills. For instance during the depression season in the U.S. in the 1930s, the depression hit the immigrants hard especially the Mexican immigrants. The depression came with food shortage, job crisis that affected every U.S. workforce, American Mexicans and Mexicans whom have to face extra challenge, which is deportation. Hostility for immigrants increased during this period, which results into the government taking drastic step that repatriate immigrants into Mexico, to which a train was provided for willing immigrants.

Shelter life and homelessness enforce great stress on immigrant parents and children asides the adaptation to the stress of the new environment and culture. Toronto records acute problem as regards affordability of shelter where housing costs are at its peak, also Toronto happens to be where immigrants settles in, thereby making immigrants face a greater risk of homelessness. However, a good understanding of the way discrimination influences homelessness among immigrant parents and their children can improve programs and public policies for immigrant parents and children as well as reduce the rate of homelessness (Emily Paradis, *et al.*, 2018).

According to a study conducted in U.S.A, it was discovered that immigrant women without status i.e. those who may be temporary workers who are awaiting the resolution of a refugee claim or wandering illegally are particularly susceptible, they often live in danger, exploitation, shelter instabilities and deep poverty. Due to the limited access to social amenities, social assistance, and other social benefits most immigrant parents especially women rely on in-house employment or the compassion of charitable organisations for shelter. Regrettably, pregnancy and childbirth signifies a crisis that affects immigrant women, which makes securing of job almost impossible as well as disrupting arrangements of housing and incurring huge healthcare costs. Relying on family shelters when there is nowhere to turn to, immigrant nursing mother are obligated to regularise their status which may unfortunately lead to their deportation when their case is considered weak by the Humanitarian and Compassionate status.

Job insecurity differs by race immigration status and ethnicity (Landsbergis, *et.al.* 2014). The risk factors for undergoing job insecurity includes being "male", i.e. the breadwinner of the family with low level of education, aged between 32 to 44 years of age and being self-employed who work in a the manufacturing sector (De Witte et. al., 2003). Unfortunately, job insecurity is linked to several emotional and physical illnesses, from anxiety, low self-esteem, and minor psychiatric symptoms to increased morbidity, musculoskeletal disorder like neck and back pains increased rates of hypertension and lastly myocardial death (Kawachi, *et. al.*, 2004). Although immigrants are more than happy to take whatever paying job that comes their way in the first few months of their entry into the new country with the hope of moving up slowly till they are comfortable which may be extremely difficult. However, immigrants who are educated find it frustrating they are not offered the opportunity to secure the job they left behind. Most times, employers prefer immigrants who gained experiences and certifications from United States, Australia, Canada, United Kingdom and New Zealand than that of other countries. As earlier pointed out in the previous chapter, the issue of language may be a major factor towards securing shelter and job and also to experience the opportunities they dreamed of experiencing in the country migrated to.

Asides being essential, having to secure safe and affordable housing is expensive. Immigrants with big family with a low paying job are most likely to live together constituting a noisy, and stressful environment, which is difficult for, kids to study or rest. Also, immigrants are prone to exploitation from their landlords and neighbours who perceive them to be gullible and unfamiliar with the societal or communal laws of their environment. For instance in Perth, a certain immigrant family was scammed by the house owner who is aware the apartment is inflicted with bedbugs and went ahead charging exorbitant fee to have the bugs exterminated.

As a family, a comfortable home with a steady paying job is imperative for the continuity of one's legacy and cultural heritage. An immigrant child is able to function properly in a home filled with love and comfort; the exemption of these will result into the regrettable suffering from emotional, psychological and physical distress. An immigrant child with no certain shelter over his or her head will surely suffer from low self-esteem and lack concentration at school. These kids are vulnerable to several paediatric psychological disorders, and if in the adolescent age, it's easier to dwindle towards drug abuse and other negative impacts associated with youthful exuberance. To curb this menace, many immigrant parents should realise when the city is densely populated with a wide gap between the low income earners and the shot callers, there is a high tendency of street life and ghetto development, therefore living in the suburbs of that host criminals is not advisable. Housing is fairly affordable and job security is semi-guaranteed based on the skill and qualification acquired.

CHAPTER 8
FEAR OF DEPORTATION

Currently, there is constant fear of immigration that lingers in the minds of both legal and illegal immigrants in Australia, Canada, and United States due to the verdict given by the home affairs minister in Australia Peter Dutton and United States presidential authority. The stress this imposes on immigrant parents and also child is intense, as it is discovered that some immigrant children have to be taught how to live as an adult at a very young age due to the fear of deportation. Deportation fear takes its toll on children as some experience psychological imbalance, from compounded tardiness, getting into fights in school and finally absence from school. There is the fear to take out their kids on a walk, or to the park, having to go to the grocery store is even a pressing issue as the fear of the unknown lingers in their minds. With the fear of deportation, their immediate environment becomes unsafe and inhabitable for them, making them prone to exploitation and insecurity. Asides that, job insecurity is also dwindling and with this fear of deportation the zeal to seek out another job is quenched, as undocumented immigrants are afraid of being exposed. Children are faced with anxiety problems as an increased number are directed to mental clinics due to lack of sleep as well as school problems caused by fear of being separated from their parents. There is the issue of peer pressure, with the rampant dissemination of information, immigrant children are susceptible to bullying from their peers who may ask them when they will be heading back to their country.

Consequently, immigrants have been told to trust the government and administration officials to do the right and civil thing, however, the act of calming immigrant and telling them not to panic is the beginning of fear itself. Particularly when there is a great reason to fear. Government integrity and persuading immigrants to trust officials is not as simple as switching off and on a typical switch and moments of deportation paints how difficult governments are to be trusted. The fear of getting deported to their homeland, immigrants are afraid to use amenities like healthcare so as not to be discovered with the information given to the healthcare system. The current administration in the United States of America triggered public health crisis among undocumented or illegal immigrants living with constant fear of deportation and relinquish medical check-up to evade being exposed. This threat placed on immigrants is not only affecting the undocumented or illegal immigrants, it also affects the legal immigrants making it difficult to use healthcare systems and adopts sponsored insurance for fear of the use of their information to deport their undocumented relatives. The immigrants prefers not to re-enrol in the subsidised health care insurance program, for instance a 58 years old Mexican woman who is a legal immigrant fears her information can be used to discover her undocumented husband which may result into separation i.e. potential deportation. Even though both the Mexican woman teenagers were born in the United States, making them citizen by birth, she is too cautious to enrol them in the subsidised health insurance. Many other immigrants have taken into this pattern, making it very difficult to live a normal life. Due to fear of deportation, many immigrants neglect vital medical assistance. This has put both the lives of parents and children in danger where undocumented immigrant waits till the illness is chronic and in acute conditions before they seek medical care, it appears some legal immigrants have copied this pattern for the fear of being noticed.

Regrettably, the fear of deportation is reflected in the lives of the immigrant's children especially those in adolescent stages. To struggle for survival the negative impact of the deportation comes with ease to them such as drug dealing, drug abuse, theft etc., this does more harm than good to them. The insecurity caused by fear of deportation has led to unhappiness and breaking of homes, as teenagers tends to channel the pain and anguish they feel deep within to either positive or negative, but judging by the fear of deportation, a larger percentage is accounted to be negative. The fear of being alone with no close relative as a teenager may contribute to the development of bad behaviours, however, if in care of social workers or voluntary caregivers, a better opportunity to curb a potential act of menace in the mind of the teenager.

The fear of deportation has portrayed the country the immigrant migrated into as a land of rightness', loneliness and loss, instead of the better opportunity they foresaw. Most schools where immigrant's children are in significant percentage end up being reduced to an island where immigrant's children draw back from. The nightmare of deportation is more real than their hopes and aspirations for being happy. Thus, making some undocumented or illegal immigrants parents in America to append their signature on the custody document of their children to a close relative in case of possible deportation to which the threat from President Donald Trump has instigated. Total number of about 11million people are said to be undocumented in America, and the American authority sees deportation as a way of depopulating the country. The pending debate between law parties is The Democrats would like to offer many of the undocumented immigrants who are non-criminal an opportunity to be citizen of the country, while the Republican argue against and supports the existing law that supports the enforcement of the law that requires the removal of undocumented immigrants. The children of immigrants find it difficult to come into terms with separation from their family, but the law is to be enforced once discovered by the officers.

Take a brief moment to picture the pain and anguish felt by human beings who fled their country in search of greener pastures in another country and unfortunately faced with the nightmare of having to steer clear off parks, clinics and public space in the bid not to get caught. Dreadful, unimaginatively Western World, right? That is how much tension many undocumented immigrants face in Australia and America today.

CHAPTER 9
OVERREPRESENTATION

The socioeconomic factors, racism and ethnic discrimination by judicial system and police, is the cause of overrepresentation in the system of criminal justice of immigrants in Western Countries. In most countries people migrate into, for instance in Norway overrepresentation is very extensive amongst family immigrants as well as individuals who are natives of African countries, however it is more complex for Asian immigrants. In essence, some Asian countries are overrepresented while some other Asian countries are underrepresented. Pertaining to offences, overrepresentation and underrepresentation pattern is also applied to different kinds of offence asides drug related offences where immigrants are underrepresented.

Also, in educational system the, Black Americans who are native to the country are not well presented in Ivy League schools. Education immigrants i.e. immigration based on studies from North America and Europe are underrepresented in Norway. According to a study conducted in 2007 by Pennsylvania and Princeton University, it records that 41% of the population of the IVY schools accounts for immigrant blacks who emigrated from African countries like Nigeria or Ghana. With this high rate of overrepresentation of black immigrants, Black Americans in Ivy League universities are being forced to redefine their blackness as well as black culture with their nationality causing disparity in amongst black students who are native born and immigrants. This leads to the raising of requests on affirmative actions as well as access to the best educational institution in America. Immigrant's kids who happen to be black in America take ample of time to get used to the different kinds of black.

The mentality and work ethic of the immigrant student may contribute to the larger percentage of black immigrants in Ivy League school like Harvard; however, most black immigrants do not consider their chances of getting into the school. Many do not consider themselves worthy of getting into the school because many consider it as not attainable. Due to the perception of many Ivy League schools that is the elitism, legacy, classism and racism, some immigrant parents often discourage their children from applying to these schools. Many immigrants are unaware of this as the general thought of America is a land of many opportunities and any chance gotten should be prudently utilised. A Nigerian Alumnus of Harvard reveals that there is a divide experience between native Black American students and Black immigrants from Africa or West Indies. Native black Americans claims that the struggle and racism faced by them are not as severe as black immigrants; this may be a result of time to which some black immigrants are only in the country to study and not experience any severe psychological impact that may affect excelling professionally or academically. The overrepresentation of immigrants and children of immigrants who are referred to as the second generation of immigrants in selective schools increases.

Child maltreatment is a risk faced by immigrant families, immigrant maltreating families are overrepresented as traditional immigrant and non-traditional immigrant that recently migrated from their countries due to hardship and political crisis, and however the overrepresentation vanished as a result of corrections based on the level of education of the traditional immigrant parents. On the other hand, non-traditional immigrant parents are still at risk for maltreatment of children still after correction for level of education. It is then advised to concentrate more on lowering the socioeconomic risks connected with the low level of education.

In Australia, it has been argued that the country's program for immigration comprises of sizeable cost to the community of Australians. This shows in part that the concern that in general that all immigrants or subgroups from recent arrivals or birthed in a particular place are in some area overrepresented in the system of social security. That explains that immigrants are more than likely to receive consistent social security payments than indigenous citizen of Australia itself, to which the clarification for it varies. A perspective to note is that immigrants are very much disadvantaged. In the sense that they are in direr need of the benefits of the payment of social security due to judgment in employment or for the reason that occupational segmentation has resulted into immigrants to be more clustered in jobs and industries susceptible to unemployment. Also, that immigrant focuses more on jobs that exposes them to risk of suffering from work-related damages to one's physical health. On the other hand, overrepresentation may lead to failures of the selection process of immigrants or of the process of settlement and related services. It may be seen from a perspective that either some particular immigrants or groups have come into being a number of culture dependency on the benefits of social security, or that there is an active exploitation experienced by immigrants of the system of social security. It has also been debated that Immigrants who migrated from countries far worse in terms of economic woes than Australia thinks of it as very logical especially under certain conditions of economic, political or social disruptions that accepts the dependence on the system of social security as an upgrading in their current state of affairs rather than as a settlement of immigrant failure (Birrel 1990; Ellard 1970). Regrettably, one of the implications to the latter perspective is that some immigrants from a certain source countries may excessively add to the outlays of social security thereby causing unwarranted burden on the Australian taxpayers.

The influence of parents is a key factor in the role model explanatory structure; it is associated with the social interaction and indicators of the children. Conferring to the views, the desire for children to imitate the success of their parents is very important so as to comprehend the process where across generation social indicators are communicated. As expected, parents with higher and quality level of education are a positive influence to the academic outcome of their child because they are positive role models to their children (Haveman, Spaulding and Wolfe, 1991). However, it is expected that children with single parents or both illiterate parents who happen to have lower level of education are likely to have less positive educational outcomes. The influence of immigrant parents as well as their aspirations has a direct impact on the performance of their children.

CHAPTER 10

ACCESS TO BASIC AMENITIES

Although in the previous chapters, we have discussed explicitly the basic necessities that immigrant's parents and their child or children need to survive in the western country hosting them. However, basic amenities such as healthcare, educational institutions, social services etc. The hardship faced by children of immigrants is the main reason most charity organisations and human services and health services programs come into contact with the family. In America, although parents may be undocumented immigrants, the children are eligible to benefit from federal aids such as Medicaid, health insurance for children, needy family temporary assistance as long as the family meets the eligibility and also meet the income guidelines. The eligibility policy differs from one state to another and most times immigrant parents not eligible. Regrettably, authorised US- citizen children with unauthorised eligible parents face a wide range of barriers towards accessing these aids or amenities due to the education and level of literacy, lack of interpretation, cultural practices and beliefs, difficulties in documenting the eligibility of the child as well as lack of transportation to offices in inaccessible locations.

The mistrust of immigrants towards agencies of public service is evidentially deepened together with heightened participation of local and state law enforcement to immigration law enforcement. The contemporary immigrant children who are between the age of 1 month to 18 year of age are diverse by settlement patterns, socioeconomic status and nationality than their parents i.e. an immigrant parent from an Asian country is referred to as Asian but his US born child will be referred to as Asian-American. The ever-increasing numbers of immigrant children correspond with a time of high inequality in socioeconomic status.

There is a cause for concern in the recent social and economic trend, almost all the social indicators indicates that children of immigrant parents perform far worse than their indigenous peers. Immigrant's children especially the youth based on research are mostly discovered to live in poverty, drop out of school, have behavioural issues and relinquish medical assistance. On the other hand, immigrant children are likely to live with both parents than the native of the country. This family arrangement is associated generally with outcomes that are beneficial for teenagers or youth than when with a single parent. Conversely, this arrangement is enfeebled for children of immigrant whose parents is not fluent in English, has minute earning capacity and authorised to work and live in the United States.

Mental and physical health status is very important in the characteristics of human capital. A poor health during childhood will result into reduced socioeconomic status in adulthood, costly workers, less productive and unhealthy workers and low income that cannot sustain their lifestyle. Consequently, the low socioeconomic status amongst immigrant parent influences the poor childhood health effects in the coming generation. Over time the stress of migration, poverty and confrontations of acculturation can significantly increase the risk of developing mental health and physical health problems. Despite these stress and challenges, the foreign-born immigrants are characterised with lower risks of morbidity and mortality than the U.S and Australian born children to parents who are immigrants. The access to amenities such as healthcare influences, physical, psychological and emotional health status.

Further to disadvantaging immigrant parents, children and young people's right to be protected from harm and socioeconomic morbidity and mortality is one of the most core fundamental human rights any parent and child must be avail with. Taking measures of action to protect them is one of the most powerful duties of any nation. Thoroughly Investigations and decision about any child thought to be at high risk of abuse or neglect are some of the most sensitive, skilled, highly-pressure and difficult professional judgments being made every day in Australian society. Such important public functions must never be open to the real, or even be perceived, risk of being done in the pursuit of profit.

Every circle of the year, the Department of Child Protection and the Police Department seized too many children from their biological parents within African Communities in Australia. Australia is regarded as a country, which had emerged from a worst child right policy to a better child right policy and more equitable child welfare system.

Immigrant parents realised that the conditions inside child foster care are terrible, and that notwithstanding the endeavours done to commend these intercessions with slogans, for example, "the best advantage of the child," Children are in danger when they are placed in a foster home care that promote inappropriate culture under Department of Child Protection. Once in a while the conditions are so unacceptable as to make the children take their own particular moves.

The issues inside of Australian's Child Protection welfare are intense, and one can't depend on the parliament and the social administrations to find the common ground for the suffering immigrants children. The Child Protection's system itself is searching for fixes that would make more employment positions inside of its own ranks - some members of African community discussed about how the system must turn out to be better at the investigations concerning the conditions the children are living under, others recommend giving the children their own particular social administrations contacts within African

Community. While the DCP system wouldn't like to give back the children to their own biological parents or particular relative homes, subsequent to these consideration situations are the exceptionally key to the enterprise booming. The DCP find their child policies as a lucrative business modal which no one or any immigrant integrity can object it mandate and the role it business environment development played.

Stopping the once used assimilation policies that were used on Aboriginal children in the earlier 1960s on African children is one of the rare dream an immigrant parent would endeavour for in Australia. The Department of Child Protection is abusing the immigrants of African communities children by imposing the inhuman regulations which are far more dangerous even the animals in the jungle would not tolerate their harsh policies on their families leave alone practising them on human children.

The government agency with its profiting partnering agencies had already torn apart and damaged the image of many families of African communities specifically the South Sudanese community.

There are staggering number of young South Sudanese children who happened to have been snatched away from their families and forced fostered to drug and alcohol addicts families who couldn't even help themselves leave alone guiding the children. Several meetings held few years ago between DCP and South Sudanese community indicates that overwhelmingly majority number of the community are fed-up with the deceiving attitudes that DCP presents. They were asked by community members to show the data of children they have under their care but they failed to comprehensively prevail accurate figures.

The Department of Child Protection and the Police Department snatched off the children from their parents promising them good life out there and protection but initially the worst cases these children encountered are:

- The children are malnourished and are in very bad health shape at DCP care
- The children are exposed to drugs, alcohol and some other illicit drugs at DCP carer

- After few weeks of the child stayed under their care, the child leaved their carer and go on the streets roaming around and until get caught by police and taken to juvenile or prison without the parents knowledge

- Most children comes out from juveniles or prisons with severe mental health illness

- Once DCP and the Police Department noticed that the child is functionless physically and mentally than he/she is dumped back to the parent to go and deal with the issue

- These two Government departments had hidden assimilation policy that is systemic racism in nature and indiscriminatingly targeting the members of African generations.

- A lot of the youth had already perished due to the psychological impact and harassment behaviours they encountered under the jurisdiction of DCP and the Police.

Is the government serious with these sort of mistreatments and harassments of this larger community?

Is this the protections the Child Protection, Police and their profiting partner organisations deem promising these young children?

The government need to invest heavily on South Sudanese youth by:

- Supporting the community base associations which are already registered, empower them to work in conjunction with government agencies which are not for profits

- Invest heavily on already established African or South Sudanese youth programs

- Introduce a better rehabilitation programs which are run by government and not-for profits South Sudanese community based organisations

- South Sudanese community in Australia lives communally in supports of each other, empower them with resourceful information and open funding support for better deed.

South Sudanese community don't really deserve this, it's a community that is serving Australia with great bright minds in different capacities. Go to the mineral sector, health sector, manufacturing sector and higher learning institutions, you would probably notice with your naked eyes that this community has produced a brilliant brains.

Due to the less chance to gain access to amenities that are essential to their well-being, poorer immigrant parents neglect the medical services needed to improve the health and lifestyle of their children. The time the care is given might be too late, as it is often given in the emergency room, and because of lack of previous medical records, this urgent medical attention may lead to high rate of child mortality. The promotion of the emotional, mental health and physical well-being of children of immigrant, policy makers as well as health professionals can eventually improve long-term the economic prospects of the coming generation. In addition, medical practitioners and health reformers and researchers should pick up more helpful hints about the children of immigrants particularly their issue of language comprehension and communication, illegal status, family partings. It helps increase the capacity of care givers and medical service providers to engage with multicultural and multilingual populace as well as continue to develop the affordability and availability of health insurance to immigrants and citizens.

It is essential and beneficial that the development of immigrant and immigrant's children is important for the integration into the Australian community else a continuous lagging will be experienced if basic amenities and policies are not reviewed and implemented. The most vital investment Australia can make is in justice system, education and healthcare institution. Even though the prospect of immigrant children is still uncertain, the most certain is the fiasco building up if major investments are not made in amenities as basic as education and healthcare system for immigrants (documented or authorised).

There will be a need to major investments that will lead to high cost of decreased tax revenues and means-tested programs in the nearest future. As the proportion of old people to workers continues to rise, laws to ensure the efficiency of prospective workers will defend on the future of the immigrant children as well as Australia is concern.

CHAPTER 11
DISCRIMINATION, STIGMATISATION AND RACISM

Minority racial and ethnic groups are susceptible to ethnic discrimination and are targeted for racism. This harmful behaviour and discriminatory attitudes may appear in different forms. On an individual level, discrimination may be felt and directly perceived as chapters of workplace discrimination, social exclusion, harassment and physical or verbal threat. Several studies have suggested that experiences of stigmatisation facing a certain racial minority or ethnic group is as a result of the identification with other immigrants or foreign-born who are defined by social class, ethnicity, gender amidst other variables to be considered.

The difference in-group status may contribute to the social context in which a person experiences discrimination. Also, the relationship to which status group occurs may modify the awareness or attributions of the causes of maltreatment of immigrant. The immigrant's place of birth or immigration status may contribute to the perception or experience of discrimination in the host country by the native-born. Although the evidence and research conducted that causes discrimination towards the relationship between immigrants based on their place of birth is still unclear, however, it contributes to the reports gathered and first-hand experiences amongst immigrant who belong to a certain ethnic or racial minority book.

Immigrant parents or immigrant persons are vulnerable and are known to experience discrimination more than Australian born persons because of the characteristics related to immigration, but also the prevailing stereotypes about the origin of their racial or ethnic group. Another form that contributes to immigrant's vulnerability to attitudes of discrimination is lack of fluency of the host country's official language and barriers in communicating more effectively for social interaction.

The social communication, lifestyle, eating habit and dressing of an immigrant significantly differs from the natives of the country and may result into exclusion or rejection by mainstreams. Immigration may heighten contact with people of several ethnic or racial groups, and may contribute to the occurrence of cross-race communications and may potentially result into the likelihood of supporting discrimination. The high rates of unemployment amongst immigrants are intensified by preconceptions on the part of their bosses against the immigrant.

This obstructs mobility upwards and weakens the capacity of the immigrant's offspring to progress economically in their life in the future. The seminar held at Bangkok circa 2000 in planning of the approaching World Conference in opposition to Xenophobia, racial discrimination, racism and other intolerable differences, the professionals noted strongly that immigration by individuals who are perceived to be very different creates tension between apparent erosion of the reliability of local culture, and labour.

One of the professionals in the conference opined that the eradication of preconception towards immigrants would prove to be complex, difficult and a long-lasting issue to resolve than institutional and legal forms of immigrant discrimination. It was established that there is imperative need for educational courses that at the final reach of the process of immigration results in the gratefulness of diversity and growth of tolerance by citizens of the host country. Also, there is a major concern for the ever increasing numbers of the children of the immigrants; they are offspring of immigrant women who may have been raped, children with mixed pedigree and children of immigrants who were/are born in the host country. These progenies are subjected to identity issues, racial discrimination as well as stigmatised often not only by the country hosting them but also the communities and countries of their nativity.

Citizen of the host country refers to immigrant persons who are stigmatised as a person who possesses undesirable difference, and stigmatisation is the moral, cultural and social processes based around apparent or supposed differences. The impact of the negative experiences of discrimination and stigmatisation is most assuredly cause adverse effects on the migrant's child or the immigrant himself or herself their sense of belonging, sexual health, self-esteem, quality of life and have been considered as sense of belonging. They also have been previously recognised as hindrances to help seeking and associated with risky behaviours.

Discrimination and stigmatisation may be experienced by migrants when accessing services such as healthcare, accommodation, employment, social exclusion and education, all of which have been identified to increase the chances of deterred or delayed help-seeking. The adverse effect of racism, stigmatisation and discrimination of immigrant's encounters further intensifies the struggle to raise children in the host country. This also accounts for a wide range of barricades in the labour market against immigrants, discrimination through skin colour, accent are restrictions linked to the status of migration, lack of recognition of language, qualification and job experience which contributes to the significant gap between natives and immigrants to which oftentimes migrants are mostly victims of exploitation. The absence of policies that integrates the inclusion as well as progression of immigrants into the labour market, which also addresses the issue of discrimination and racial status, it will consistently result into difficult plights for radicalised immigrants.

Progressing the protection of migrants in the face of discrimination, racism hostility and stigmatisation of their human rights demands strategies, approaches and organisation as well as the ability to mobilise material resources and manpower. Government institutions and officials, civil society establishments, international organisations and immigrant groups of ethnic or racial minority all have major contributions to make and roles to take. Several schemes and wits described in this chapter demonstrate that cooperation and dialogue is viable and possible amongst corporate and international, governmental and civil society.

All these bodies and more will be needed to come up with unconventional solutions, contribute to the amplification or explanation of national policies, influence the development and progress of events and many more. When developing a rights-based tactic, it needs to be adequately incorporated in activities and policies of international organisations especially in the cooperation and assistance they provide to government. The lack of political wills is a major issue that can make the modification between effective interventions to challenge discrimination and racism or the continuous exposure of migrants to its effect. The dignity and rights of all immigrants as well as their children should be respected so as to avoid repeating racial and xenophobic mistakes of past times.

CHAPTER 12
CULTURAL EXPECTATIONS

Migrants and their children are sure to face different forms of challenges to help adapt to their new environment and the culture. In previous chapters, we have addressed most of the issues migrant families living in the western countries in relation to their adaptation and comfort. Most immigrant parents are just focused mainly on the better opportunities of the destination country and are not paying too much cognisance of cultural expectations that has potential risk of clash and conflicts within the family. Take for instance, most African and Asian countries are very keen on respect, with different modes and forms of greeting and showing reverence to superiors and family, it may seem strange to peers or fellow neighbours in the host western countries.

Challenges faced due to cultural expectations is the potential intra-family clash, i.e. when the child of the immigrant seem to be more comfortable and takes in the host country's culture appreciatively than that of the parent. This problem is more pressing especially in cases of teenagers when the socialisation between friends of the opposite gender from other culture, the child begins to raise issues of social rights and freedom, parents are bothered about academic performance and rapid rate of westernization in their child.

Considering the sacrifices taken up by the migrant parents to provide shelter and a better opportunity as opposed to what will be given in their home country, migrant parents consider it disrespectful when their children do not appreciate the compromise and sacrifices endured to provide them with better opportunity in the host country.

This is as a result of adaptation of the child to the foreign odd and strange cultures so rapidly. For the female gender especially teenage girls, the migrant parents are much more concerned with the risk of young pregnancy as well as their well-being. Also, strong admonition in regards to dressing, interaction and socialising with friends of the opposite gender, deportment with the opposite gender with regards of the time and place are more stressed in females than males. Except the risk of pregnancy that reduces the scrutiny placed by migrant parent, male children of the migrant also face cultural necessities as well as conflicts.

Nevertheless, they are subjected to high pressure of academic excellence, which may or may not settle well with them. If the reception of the pressure is not taken well, the male child may reject the culture of the family, and easily be a victim of illusions of freedom from authority by sinking into gangs or counter-culture groups. This will in turn lead to the risk of conflict with abject academic failure and extreme conflict with the family and law of the host country.

The major challenge is how the parents will adapt and find logical strategies to influence cultural expectations in the perspective of a greater possibility that their children will be changed by the culture of the host country. The major question is how and to what extent the migrant children will be changed by the new culture. In addition, some parents may be from cultures where it is a norm to instruct a child on what to do and demand total obedience. These wear away quickly from kids raised and socialised in the culture of the western world where freedom of each person is rewarded and respected. Therefore, it is imperative for the parents with control strategies to adjust and come up with strategies that minimalize the risk of conflict with their kids and also have the opportunity to still be a major influence to them.

Just as dialogue is the best weapon to curb war, sharing stories that explains reasons why parents chose to migrate to the host country as well as their aspirations and dreams for the future of the family can yield more positive results than nagging. Also, when parents encourage their kids to engage in an information flow about the disparity between their respective lives non-judgmentally, children and parents may be apprised of their respective involvements and may further benefit them into a better position to discuss disparity between themselves as a family.

The issue here is for the immigrant parents to acquire skills that depend more upon encouragement than control. This can be simplified and aided by participation and appreciation of cultural activities and inviting their children's new friends to participate. Deciding together with your children their nature of friends can be a better way of sustaining honesty than segregating from friends. Oftentimes children of immigrants are often faced with internal conflicts that may culturally split in trying to be a compliant and obedient child at home and host country savvy in school. This results into living a double life, which can be too stressing to the child, as there is a potential lost in identity.

Below are few helpful tips that parents and professionals can adopt to influence communication and settle conflicts. They include;

- Immigrant Parents should physically show their encouragement and appreciation rather than disapproval and disappointment.
- Parents should enquire about their experience and beliefs not with a judgmental tone but out of mere curiosity.
- Parents should plan and minimise overbreeding their families to avoid disengagement of their children; an affordable family does prosper without hindrance in child's assurance of support.
- Consistent times for conversations and interaction should be set as parents.

- Parents and their children can develop the act of listening to each other to understand and not only to respond, it helps to recognise and understand where there is lapses in cultural differences. This process requires willingness and openness of both parties.

These results of these hints are helpful and apparent when applied on a regular basis with lots of patience and perseverance. Parents should be conscious and sensitive to this improve but overall patient with their kids when applying these hints.

CONCLUSION

All the chapters in this book pointed majorly to "unimaginatively western world" the unpreparedness of the immigrant either documented or undocumented, as well as the challenges they face most especially migrants with children. It is rather stressful to compromise and make major sacrifices to cross the border of one's country to another in search of better opportunities, only to be faced with several nightmares that are detrimental to survival. Asides gaining entry into the host country either lawfully or through the 'back door', it is essential to note that the reception of native born is dependent on several other factors with language barrier being the most important in order to aid better communication and interaction. Except migration is based on job opening, it is quite difficult for job security and shelter, this hardship is mostly experienced by undocumented immigrants. The compassion of the government and other charity agencies is mostly to the children of immigrants as most suffer from malnutrition, starvation and disease that are associated with paediatrics. Regrettably, the parents of the immigrants wait till this illness are at the chronic stage before consulting medical aid, this is due to the constant fear of deportation to their native country or isolation from their children. Another major issue faced by legal or documented immigrant is discrimination, this is due to the perceived news apparent to their native country i.e. some African and Asian countries have been known to instigate terrorism, cyber theft, kidnapping etc. This discrimination hinders the comfort and liberty of the migrant within the society and this can be harmful to the kids making them vulnerable to physical attacks, bullying or emotional stability. Essentially, most immigrant parents should communicate effectively with their children as they are young at heart and in wit to understand and withstand the pressures the new environment impose on them.

The End…of Unimaginatively Western World!

Reference
1. U.S. Bureau of the Census, 2015 American Community Survey One-Year Estimates. Selected Characteristics of the Native and Foreign-Born Populations. The cited figures are for adults 25 years old and older. Retrieved from the website of the American Fact Finder.
2. McLeod, J.D. and Shanashan, M.J., (1993). Poverty, Parenting, and Children's Mental Health. AM Social Rev. 58:351-366.
3. Devine, J.A., Plunkett, M., and Wright, J.D. (1992). The chronicity of poverty: evidence from the PSID, 1968-1987. Soc Forces. 70:787-812.
4. Roberto S., Jill, H.W., and Audrey S. (2011). Immigration and Poverty in American Suburbs. Metropolitan Policy Program. 1-21.
5. Portes A. Lost in translation: Language Acquisition and loss in the United States. Spanish in the US Conference has been held in conjunction with the Spanish in Contact with Other Languages Conference.

6. Gleason, J.B. (1997). The development of language. 4. Needham Heights, MA: Allyn & Bacon.
7. Emily Paradis, Sylvia Novac, Monica Sarty and Hulchanski, J.D. (2008). Better Off in a Shelter? Centre for Urban and Community Studies. 1-8pp.
8. De Witte, H. and Naswall, K., (2003). "Who feels insecure in Europe? Predicting job insecurity from background variables", Economic and Industrial Democracy, vol. 24, no. 2, pp. 189-215.
9. Landsbergis, P. A., Grzywacz, J.G., and Lamontagne, A. D., (2014). "Work organization, job insecurity, and occupational health disparities." American journal of Industrial Medicine, vol. 57, no. 5 pp. 495-515.
10. Kawach, I., Lee, S., Colditz, G. A. and Berkman, L.F. 2004."Prospective study of job insecurity and coronary heart disease in US women", Annals of Epidermology, vol.14, no. 1, pp. 24-30.
11. https://www.theatlantic.com/health/archive/2017/03/deportation-stress/520008/

12. https://tonic.vice.com/en_us/article/a3n995/legal-immigration-healthcare-deportation-fears
13. www.bbc.co.uk/news/world-us-canada-40600552
14. https://www.theroot.com/black-immigrants-overrepresented-in-the-ivy-league-1790869651
15. https://www.npr.org/templates/story/story.php?storyId=10080304
16. Peter Whiteford, (1991). Are Immigrants Overrepresented in the Australian Social Security System? Journal of the Australian Population Association. Vol.8, No.2. 93-94pp.
17. Birrell, R. 1990. The Chains that Bind: Family Reunion Migration to Australia in the 1980s.
18. Ellard, J. 1970. Psychological reaction to compensable injury. Medical Journal of Australia 2, August 22:349–355.
19. Marta Tiennda and Ron Haskins, 2011. Immigrant Children: Introducing the Issue. The Future of Children. Vol.21, No.1.
20. http://www.un.org/WCAR/e-kit/migration.htm
21. Aggleton P., Parker R., Maluwa M. Stigma, Discrimination, and HIV/AIDS in Latin America

and the Caribbean. Inter-American Development Bank; Washington, DC, USA: 2003.
22. Pescosolido B., Martin J. The stigma complex. Annu. Rev. Sociol. 2015; 41:87–116. doi: 10.1146/annurev-soc-071312-145702.
23. https://www.socialworkhelper.com/2017/02/01/issues-immigrant-parents-children/
24. https://conflictremedy.com/culture-clash-immigrant-parents-and-their-teens/
25. https://ses.library.usyd.edu.au/bitstream/2123/1209/5/05chapter4.pdf
26. Http___www.aphref.aph.gov.au_house_committee_jfadt_africa%2009_report_chapter%208-africans%20in%20autralia.pdf
27. Adepoju, A., 1997. 'Family, Population and Development in Africa'. Zed Book Ltd., London.
28. Findley, S., 1997. 'Migration and Family Interaction in Africa' in Adepoju, A. (ed), 'Family, Population and Development in Africa'. Zed Book Ltd, London.

29. Jakubowicz, A., 2010. 'Australia Migration Policies: African Dimensions', Background Paper for African Australians: A Review of Human Rights and Social Inclusion Issues.
30. https://www.theguardian.com/commentisfree/2016/mar/08/stereotyping-of-africans-is-everywhere-but-australians-are-particularly-clueless
31. Browne, D. (2005) Ethnic Minorities, Electronic Media, and the Public Sphere: A Comparative Study. Cresskill, NJ: Hampton Press. Cover, R. (2012) „Digital transitions: Minority Ethnic Community Media, Local/Home Hybridity, and Digitization of the means of Communication", Australian Journal of Communication 39(2): 19-33.
32. Budarick, J., and Gil-Soo Han. 2013. The importance of ethnic minority media: African-Australian media.
33. https://www.thesaturdaypaper.com.au/news/media/2017/02/25/race-stereotyping-and-melbournes-apex-gang/14879412004275

34. https://theconversation.com/mistreating-minorities-victoria-police-and-racial-profiling-12307
35. Colic-Peisker V & Tilbury F 2005, Refugees and employment: The Effects of Visible Difference on Discrimination, Centre for Social and Community Research, Murdoch University, Perth.
36. Colic-Peisker V & Tilbury F 2006, 'Employment niches for recent refugees. Segmented labor market in 21st Century Australia', Journal of Refugee Studies, vol. 19, pp. 203–29.
37. Human Rights and Equal Opportunity Commission HREOC 1991, Racist violence: Report Of the National Inquiry into Racist Violence in Australia, HREOC, AGPS, Canberra.
38. Human Rights and Equal Opportunity Commission HREOC 1999, New Country New Stories: Discrimination and Disadvantage Experienced by People in Small and Emerging Communities, HREOC, Sydney.
39. Szalacha LA, Erkut S, García Coll C, Fields JP, Alarcón O & Ceder I 2003, 'Perceived

discrimination and resilience', in SS Luthar (ed.), Resilience and vulnerability: Adaptation in the context of childhood adversities, Cambridge University Press, pp. 414–35.

40. Caughy MO, O'Campo PJ & Muntaner C 2004, 'Experiences of racism among African American parents and the mental health of their preschool-aged children', American Journal of Public Health, vol. 94, pp. 2118–24.

41. Mays VM, Cochran SD & Barnes NW 2007, 'Race, Race-Based Discrimination, and Health Outcomes Among African Americans', Annual Review of Psychology, vol. 58, no. 1, pp. 201–25.

42. Dunn K, Forrest J, Pe-Pua R & Smith S 2005, 'Experiences of Racism in the Australian Body Politic: Extent, Spheres, and Cultural Unevenness', in T Khoo (ed.), The Body Politic: Racialised Political Cultures in Australia, refereed proceedings from the University of Queensland Australian Studies Centre Conference, Brisbane, 24–26 November 2004, University of Queensland

Australian Studies Centre and Monash University National Centre for Australian Studies.

43. https://theconversation.com/heres-how-minority-job-seekers-battle-bias-in-the-hiring-process-43897

44. https://www.vichealth.vic.gov.au/-/.../ResearchSummary_Discrimination.pdf?la=en...

45. https://www.theguardian.com/australia-news/2018/jan/03/is-melbourne-in-the-grip-of-african-gangs-the-facts-behind-the-lurid-headlines

46. http://www.abc.net.au/news/2018-01-17/what-statistics-tell-us-about-melbournes-african-crime-issue/9336604

47. https://www.theguardian.com/australia-news/2018/jan/06/were-not-a-gang-the-pain-of-being-african-australian

48. https://www.sbs.com.au/news/melbourne-could-take-lead-from-sydney-on-youth-crime-problem-sudanese-refugee-says

www.ingramcontent.com/pod-product-compliance
Lightning Source LLC
Chambersburg PA
CBHW032141040426
42449CB00005B/352